Rewired

Relearning Parenting
beyond The Typical
and Reconnecting
The Village

AMELIA BRAY

Copyright © 2025 Amelia Bray

All rights reserved.

No part of this publication may be reproduced, stored in a retrieval system, or transmitted in any form or by any means—electronic, mechanical, photocopying, recording, or otherwise—without the prior written permission of the author, except for brief quotations used in reviews or scholarly works.

This publication is for informational and inspirational purposes only. It is not intended as a substitute for professional medical, therapeutic, or legal advice. Always seek the guidance of qualified professionals with any questions or concerns you may have regarding your child's development or personal circumstances.

For permissions, collaboration, or questions, please contact

Amelia_skylark@outlook.com

@Amelia_Skylark

Acknowledgements

Writing this book has been an emotional and personal journey, and I couldn't have brought it to life without the support and encouragement from a few key people.

To those who read early drafts ... thank you for your honesty, your time and your willingness to sit with these words while they were still finding form. Your feedback and insight helped shape this book into something real and meaningful.

To my husband ... your daily strength, patience and commitment are the quiet force behind everything I do. You show up every day with maximum effort and it never goes unnoticed.

And to my children ... you are my greatest teachers. Your unique ways of seeing the world inspire me endlessly. Thank you for always reminding me what truly matters. Sharing this lifetime together ... even when its hard ... is the greatest privilege I will ever know.

This book is for all of you. With love and gratitude.

Introduction: A Letter to the Whole Village

For those parenting, loving, and walking beside an autistic child.

This book is born from lived experience … raw, reshaped, and rewired by the journey of loving an autistic child. If you are holding this in your hands, you may be a parent navigating unknowns, a grandparent searching for understanding, a friend wanting to say the right thing, or someone who simply loves deeply and wants to do better.

Wherever you stand, you belong here.

When I first began writing, I planned to create two separate books … one for parents and caregivers, and another for extended family and friends. But somewhere along the way, it struck me deeply that separation is part of the very disconnection we're trying to heal. The idea that we each need our own version of the truth is part of what keeps us apart. And so, this became one book of two parts … because connection begins with shared understanding.

Part One is a compassionate, honest space for parents and caregivers … those in the thick of it, learning to let go of the typical and build something just as beautiful, if not more so. It's where grief and growth often hold hands. It's where fatigue meets fierce love.

Part Two is for the wider circle … the family members, friends, teachers, and kind-hearted souls who want to support, but may feel unsure how. It's a gentle guide into the world we inhabit, and a loving invitation to come closer, not step back.

But I want to gently encourage you … read it all. Read the parts "meant" for someone else. Walk beside the parent in Part One. Sit with the outsider's good intentions in Part Two. When we see through each other's eyes, even briefly, we create room for real connection.

This is not a manual or a manifesto. It's a collection of truths … some tender, some tired, many still unfolding. It's a space to be seen, to feel held, and maybe to exhale for the first time in a while.

Thank you for being here. Thank you for choosing to love, to learn, and to rewire the way we see the world … and each other.

With love,

Amelia

REWIRED

Relearning Parenthood
beyond the Typical

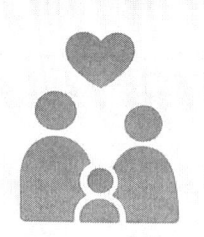

AMELIA BRAY

Introduction

This book was born from quiet moments of exhaustion, hope, reflection, and fierce love. As a parent of a child on the autism spectrum, you carry a weight that few understand unless they've walked this path themselves. This book isn't here to fix things, or offer tidy solutions. It's here to be a companion … to remind you that you are not alone. It is possible to feel broken and brave at the same time. This is for the sleepless nights, the small wins, the invisible strength, and the deep inner transformation that comes from parenting differently-wired children. May these pages feel like a hand on your shoulder, or a voice saying, "Me too."

I see you.
I see the tired eyes that still light up with love.
I see the questions swirling in your mind … "Am I doing enough?" "Am I getting this right?"
I see the strength that doesn't always feel like strength, and the quiet courage it takes to wake up each day and show up again.
This book isn't here to give you rules or solutions. It's not a checklist or a manual.

It's a hand on your shoulder. A hug.

A deep breath in the middle of the storm. It's a reminder that you are not alone in this journey.
Parenting a child on the autism spectrum asks more of you … more patience, more flexibility, more emotional resilience.
But it also *gives* you more … more insight, more compassion, more connection than you ever imagined possible.
This book is made up of reflections. Of moments you might recognise. Of things I wish someone had told me.
You won't find perfection here. But you will find honesty. And hope.
Let's begin this journey together. One chapter, one deep breath, one loving step at a time.

A Letter from One Parent to Another

Dear You,

If you're reading this, you're probably in the thick of it … raising, loving, and learning alongside a child on the autism spectrum. Maybe today was a hard day. Maybe you're exhausted, confused, overwhelmed, or even feeling guilty for not "enjoying every moment." I've been there.

This isn't a guide full of perfect solutions or sugar-coated stories. This is a space where the real, raw, and beautiful parts of parenting an autistic child are all allowed to exist together. The chaos and the calm. The heartbreak and the joy. The resilience and the rebirth.

It's Okay to Cry and Still Be Strong.
This life isn't easy. It's also rich in meaning, depth, and transformation. You're doing a job most people couldn't even begin to understand … and you're doing it with love. Let this be your reminder that you are *seen*, *valued*, and *growing*, even on the days you feel like you're standing still.

Raising a child with autism doesn't just change your life … it changes *you*. It challenges who you thought you were, and then invites you to become something stronger, softer, and more deeply human.

Let's walk through this together.

With love and understanding,

Amelia xxx

Contents

1. When the World Shifts

2. The Weight of Invisible Work

3. The Gifts They Give Us

4. You Are Not Failing

5. Your Intuition is Powerful. Trusting Yourself as the Expert on Your Child.

6. Building a Life That Works for You

7. Connection over Compliance

8. The Road Ahead

9. When the Village Doesn't Show Up

10. Permission to Rest. Why Self-Compassion is Vital.

11. Filling your cup when you have no Village.

Final note

Chapter 1: When the World Shifts

There's a moment that changes everything. It might come suddenly, in a sterile room with a doctor delivering the words, "Your child is on the autism spectrum." Or it might come slowly, after months (or years) of noticing things others didn't seem to see ... how your child moves, reacts, speaks, or doesn't.

And in that moment, the world tilts.

You may feel relief. You may feel grief. You might feel validated, scared, overwhelmed ... or everything at once. You're not alone in that. Every feeling is valid. Every reaction is normal.

> *"You can have a diagnosis day and a mourning day, and a 'let's do this' day all in the same week. Parenting doesn't follow a script—it follows your heart."*
> — Autism Mum

We often expect that parenting will look a certain way. We imagine milestones, family outings, playground laughs, and school photos. But autism parenting doesn't fit neatly into anyone's idea of "typical." It's messier, deeper, and more complex. And while that might shake your world at first, it also opens you up to a new kind of beauty.

The Grief That's Hard to Talk About

No one talks enough about the silent grief that comes after a diagnosis. It's not grief for your child ... your child is exactly who they're meant to be. It's the grief for all the assumptions you unknowingly carried. The "shoulds." The "what ifs." The comparison to other children, other families, other paths.
That grief doesn't make you a bad parent. It makes you a human one.

> *"Grief is not a betrayal of your child. It's the breaking of the boxes you were handed. And when the boxes break, so does your old idea of what 'normal' should look like."*
> — From the journal of a parent, one month post-diagnosis

Finding Your Feet on New Ground

Once the initial wave settles, you start to adapt ... often without realizing it. You learn new words like "regulation," "sensory seeking," "masking." You begin to notice the little things your child does that others might miss—the way they flap their hands when excited, or the comfort they find in patterns and predictability. You become their translator, their advocate, their protector. You build your life around what works for *them*, even if it means reshaping everything you knew before.

And slowly, the world shifts again—this time not in shock, but in understanding.

> *"I stopped asking, 'Why is this happening?' and started asking, 'What can this teach me?' That's when everything changed."*
> — Autism Dad, after 3 years of home education

Reflection Prompt:
Take a moment to write down or think about the moment everything shifted for you.

1. What emotions came up?

2. What assumptions did you have to let go of?

3. What strengths did you discover in yourself during that time?

You might cry. You might laugh. You might feel proud of how far you've come. Hold space for it all. This is your story too.

Chapter 2: The Weight of Invisible Work

There's a kind of work you can't put on a to-do list. No one sees it, but it's always there ... buzzing in the background of your mind like a never-ending taskbar. This is the **invisible work** of parenting a child on the spectrum.

It's the scanning of environments for sensory triggers before you even step inside.

It's pre-planning every meal, every outing, every bedtime routine like a military operation.

It's holding it together during the meltdowns and holding it *all in* when strangers stare.

It's researching at 2 a.m. whether your child's new food refusal is sensory, developmental, or just a phase.

You don't get a paycheck for this work. There's no promotion. No coffee break. And often, no one claps for you at the end of the day. But make no mistake ... it's *real*, essential work. And you are doing it.

> *"It's the kind of work that doesn't get seen, but if you stopped doing it, everything would fall apart."*
> — Special needs parent reflection

The Loneliness of Advocacy

You may find yourself fighting for things that should come easily. Support at school. Referrals. Understanding. Even simple compassion. You learn to use your

voice when you'd rather be quiet. You become the expert, the advocate, the admin assistant, the care coordinator.
And often, you're doing it *alone* … even if you're not technically alone.
Friends may drift away. Extended family might not "get it."

Professionals might question your parenting. You'll hear things like:
- "All kids do that sometimes."
- "He just needs more discipline."
- "You're overthinking it."

And each time, you swallow the lump in your throat and carry on.
Because you know your child better than anyone. And because love makes you fierce.

"She doesn't talk yet, but I still hear her. I hear what she needs. And I fight for it."
— Mother of a non-speaking child, age 4

You Are Not 'Too Sensitive'

The world may label you difficult, emotional, dramatic. You've likely been told you're "overreacting" or "making a big deal out of nothing." But what they don't understand is that you've had to become hyper-aware … for your child's safety, well-being, and dignity.

Your sensitivity is your strength. It's what allows you to notice the slightest change in their body language. To sense a meltdown brewing from a flicker in their eyes. To know when a situation is too much … before the storm comes.

"We are not broken. We are just operating at a higher level of awareness, because that's what our children need from us."
— Autism parent advocate

Reflection Prompt:

What parts of your work as a parent go unseen by others, but take up the most energy?

1. Is it emotional, like worry or guilt?

2. Is it mental, like planning, researching, or anticipating?

3. Is it relational, like feeling misunderstood by family, friends, or professionals?

You are carrying more than most people will ever know … and you're doing it with love. That matters. You matter.

Chapter 3: The Gifts They Give Us

It's easy to get lost in the noise of therapy goals, meltdowns, sleepless nights, and the weight of responsibility. But if you pause for just a moment ... if you lean in ... you'll start to see something extraordinary taking shape:

Your child is teaching you.

Not in the way a teacher holds a chalkboard or a coach calls from the sidelines—but in the way the *soul* teaches. Quietly. Subtly. Deeply. Through presence, through difference, and through a kind of wisdom that isn't learned in books.

Slowing Down to the Beauty in the Details

Before this journey, life probably felt fast. Rushed mornings, busy afternoons, endless expectations.

Now, you've learned to **slow down** ... because your child taught you how. You've learned to see the wonder in repetitive moments, the beauty in the quiet, and the joy in a single sound, movement, or look that once might've gone unnoticed.

Maybe your child spent half an hour lining up toy animals. Maybe they played with water beads for so long you thought they'd melt into the floor. And instead of rushing them on, you stayed. You watched. And something inside you softened.

> *"My son taught me that joy doesn't need to be big or loud. It can live in the small, sacred spaces where stillness is allowed to exist."*
> — Mum of an 8-year-old with ASD

Rediscovering the World Through Their Eyes

You see life differently now.

You've learned that **communication isn't always verbal**, but it's still real. That eye contact isn't the only way to connect. That play doesn't have to look like everyone else's. That stimming isn't a "problem" … it's expression.

You've stopped needing your child to "fit in," and started learning how to **meet them where they are**.

You've watched them light up at things no one else noticed … a shadow dancing on the wall, a crack in the pavement, the hum of a radiator. You've come to understand that there is no *one* way to experience the world. And suddenly, *your world has expanded too.*

> *"Before, I looked at the world. Now I look with him. And it's more colourful than I ever imagined."*
> — Dad of a sensory-seeking child

Learning What Love Really Means

Your love has been tested in fire and it has held.

You have loved through shutdowns and meltdowns, through misunderstandings and hospital visits, through late-night Googling and early-morning tears.

And still, you love. Fiercely. Unconditionally. With every ounce of strength you didn't even know you had.

There is a kind of love that autism parenting demands … a love that doesn't require your child to change in order to be celebrated. That love lives in you now.

"I used to think I had to 'fix' everything. Now I just want to honour who my child is—and love them so well they never doubt it."
— Parent of a newly diagnosed teen

Reflection Prompt:
What has your child taught you—about the world, about yourself, about love?

1. What do you notice now that you never did before?

2. In what ways has your heart grown since beginning this journey?

Write it down. Hold it close. These lessons are your legacy, too.

Chapter 4: You Are Not Failing

Let's be honest … some days feel like complete chaos.

The routine breaks, the meltdown hits, the phone rings, the dishes pile up, and you can't remember the last time you showered, let alone felt like you were doing a "good job." You go to bed with a racing mind, replaying what you could have done differently, wondering if you're enough.

And if no one has told you this lately … let me say it clearly:

You. Are. Not. Failing.

You are parenting in a reality most people will never understand. And you are doing it with courage, love, and a kind of strength that doesn't always look like success … but *is*.

The Myth of the Perfect Parent

Somewhere along the way, we were handed a silent script that said "a good parent" always knows what to do. That they stay calm, keep a clean house, follow every professional's advice, and never cry in the bathroom.

But let's rip that script up right now.
The truth is:

- Good parents lose their temper.
- Good parents sometimes let their kids eat toast three meals in a row.
- Good parents cry when it gets too heavy.
- Good parents *don't always have the answers*.

Especially when parenting a child on the autism spectrum.
There is no manual for this. You are writing one, day by day, from scratch.

> *"Some days I feel like I'm barely keeping it together. But then I look at how safe and loved my child feels—and I remember, that's what matters most."*
> — Autism parent, 5 years post-diagnosis

The Quiet Cost of Compassion Fatigue

Caring for others while constantly pushing your own needs aside? That's a recipe for burnout.
You might feel numb, emotionally drained, or disconnected from your own identity. You may even feel resentment … and then guilt for feeling it.
This isn't a personal flaw. It's called **compassion fatigue**, and it's real.
You're not broken. You're depleted. And what you need isn't shame or judgment … it's **nourishment**. Space. Support. Permission to stop holding it all together for just a moment.

"I thought if I stopped, everything would fall apart. But when I paused—just for me—I realized I wasn't the one falling apart. I was just carrying too much alone."
— Mum of two, including one autistic teen

What If Showing Up Is the Win?

Not every day needs to be productive.
Not every moment has to be a teaching moment.
Sometimes, surviving the day is the **highest form of success**.
Did you show up with love today?
Did you make one safe space?
Did you try your best … even if it didn't look like your best yesterday?

That's enough. You're enough.

―――――

Reflection Prompt:
In what ways do you judge yourself too harshly? What would you say to a friend who was doing everything you're doing now?

1. Would you call her a failure, or would you remind her how strong and selfless she is?

2. Try speaking to yourself with that same compassion.

You are raising a child in a world that doesn't always understand them … and doing it with more grace than you know. This isn't failure. This is **heroism in slow motion.**

Chapter 5: Your Intuition is Powerful. Trusting Yourself as the Expert on Your Child.

There's something sacred about the connection between a parent and their child. When your child is neurodivergent, that connection can become even more finely tuned … because you learn to listen differently. You observe the world through their eyes. You become fluent in a language no one taught you.

And yet, despite this deep bond and lived experience, many parents of SEND children find themselves second-guessing their instincts. Perhaps it's the weight of professionals' opinions. Maybe it's the endless online noise. Or perhaps it's the well-meaning (but often unhelpful) advice from others who don't walk in your shoes.

But here's the truth:

You are the expert on your child.

You are the one who notices the subtle shifts in their mood before they speak a word.

You are the one who's studied their triggers, their comforts, their "tells."

You are the one who lies awake at night wondering what more you can do.

You are the one who advocates fiercely, relentlessly—even when your voice shakes.

No degree, diagnosis, or textbook can override the thousands of moments you've lived alongside your child. The sleepless nights. The quiet breakthroughs. The meltdowns. The triumphs. The times you've had to fight through red tape or misunderstanding just to be heard.

There will be moments when you feel dismissed, misunderstood, or patronised. There will be professionals who don't listen closely enough … or who try to box your child into a chart or checklist. In those moments, it can be tempting to shrink. To doubt yourself. To wonder if you're just "being dramatic" or "too emotional."

But don't.

Hold your ground.

Ask the awkward questions.

Push back with grace when needed.

Say no when something doesn't feel right.

Say yes when your heart knows what your child needs.

Intuition is not guesswork. It's lived knowledge. It's informed by every moment of connection, observation, and care. It's a blend of wisdom, experience, and deep emotional knowing.

Trusting yourself doesn't mean rejecting support—it means partnering with it from a place of confidence, not submission. It means inviting professionals into your world, not the other way around.

So the next time you feel that gut feeling—when something seems off, or something lights your child up in a beautiful way—lean into it. Your intuition is a compass. It's not perfect, but it's powerful. And it's yours.

You were never "just" a parent.

You've always been the anchor.

The translator.

The protector.

The guide.

And your child is better for it.

Reflection Prompt: Trusting My Inner Knowing

Take a few quiet moments to reflect on your unique connection with your child. You might like to write your answers in a journal, speak them aloud, or simply sit with them in your heart.

1. Describe a time when you just knew something about your child before anyone else did.
   What did your intuition tell you? How did you respond?
2. Have you ever doubted yourself because of another person's opinion or advice?
3. What helped you find your way back to your truth?
4. What signs or "tells" do you recognise in your child that others might miss?
   (Think about their body language, tone, energy shifts, or needs.)
5. What would it feel like to fully trust your intuition—even when it goes against the grain?
   Visualise what that version of you looks and sounds like.
6. Finish this sentence:
   I am the expert on my child because...

Chapter 6: Building a Life That Works for You

When your child is diagnosed, the world doesn't hand you a map. It hands you a maze … one filled with appointments, acronyms, systems, and experts who often contradict one another.

And somewhere in that chaos, you start to ask **"What if we did things our way?"**

That question can feel terrifying at first … like you're walking away from what's "normal." But in time, it becomes empowering. Because building a life that works for your family may not look traditional … but it can be full of connection, peace, and joy.

Permission to Break the Rules

You're allowed to decline the parties, skip the loud school assemblies, or say "no" to things that cause your child unnecessary distress. You're allowed to turn down professionals who don't listen. You're allowed to walk out of places that aren't safe, inclusive, or kind.

You are allowed to do what works … even if it doesn't make sense to anyone else.

> *"We pulled our son out of mainstream school. People thought we were ruining his future. What we were really doing was giving him back his peace."*
> — Home-educating mum of an 11-year-old autistic boy

The Courage to Create Your Own Rhythm

Your daily life may look very different now.

It might include:
- Therapy sessions or sensory play in the middle of the day
- Long walks with noise-cancelling headphones
- Meal routines that look the same, every single week
- Quiet birthdays at home instead of big parties

And that's not failure. That's *design*. That's **intentional parenting** based on who your child really is ... not who society expects them to be.

Some families thrive with structure. Others need space to be spontaneous. Some children need constant sensory input. Others need a calm, low-stimulation environment. The beauty is: *you get to choose what works*.

> "I stopped chasing 'normal' and started chasing 'peaceful.' Everything got better after that."
> — Autism parent, UK

Redefining Success

Let's redefine success ... not as perfect outcomes, but as authentic connection.

Success might look like:
- A meltdown prevented because you noticed early signs
- A smile in a moment that would've once been scary
- A day where your child felt safe in their skin
- You, giving yourself grace and breathing a little deeper than yesterday

Those moments don't make headlines, but they build a beautiful life.

"Progress isn't always visible. Sometimes it's in the quiet moments. The calm after the storm. The eye contact. The trust."
— Reflection from a mum of a non-verbal 6-year-old

Reflection Prompt:
What have you let go of in order to build a more peaceful, authentic life? What expectations no longer serve your child—or you?

1. What routines, choices, or adaptations have brought your family *more ease*?

2. How can you celebrate those choices instead of apologising for them?

You are not behind. You are not off-track.

You are **exactly where you need to be** … creating a life tailored to the child you love.

Chapter 7: Connection Over Compliance

There's a loud message in parenting culture that says "good behaviour" equals success.

Sit still. Follow instructions. Make eye contact. Don't interrupt. Say please and thank you.

But when you parent a child on the spectrum, those expectations can feel more like *walls* than goals. And slowly, you begin to realise: **compliance doesn't equal connection** … and connection is what matters most.

Shifting the Lens

Your child might not say "I love you" in words … but they show it in glances, gestures, in the way they seek your presence during their hardest moments. They may not want hugs, but they let you into their world through shared interests, through rhythm and repetition, through simply existing beside you.

You've learned that your child isn't "disobedient" or "rude" … they're communicating in the language of *neurodiversity*.

And with that lens, everything changes.

> *"Once I stopped trying to fix the way she interacted, and started joining her where she was, we both began to breathe easier."*
> — Parent of a 5-year-old with ASD

When 'Compliance' Hurts More Than It Helps

There are moments when the world asks your child to behave in ways that simply aren't possible for them … at least not without distress or masking.

They're told to:
- Make eye contact when it's painful
- Sit still when their body *needs* to move
- Tolerate loud rooms when they're overwhelmed
- Be quiet when they're stimming to self-regulate

And when they can't, they're told they're difficult.

But you know better. You know their behaviour is a form of expression, a way of saying "This is too much," or "I don't feel safe," or "I need help." And when you choose to honour that instead of suppress it … you're teaching your child that they're **not broken**.

> *"He used to get punished at school for leaving the room. At home, I let him walk away and he comes back when he's ready. That's trust. That's growth."*
> — Father of a sensory-avoidant child

Connection Builds Safety, and Safety Builds Growth

When a child feels *safe*, their nervous system begins to settle. Their capacity to engage, to learn, to try new things increases … not because they're forced, but because they feel secure.

This kind of trust isn't built through reward charts or rigid rules. It's built through presence. Through staying calm during storms. Through offering comfort instead of punishment. Through saying, "I see you ... and you're okay."

> "My daughter doesn't need to be fixed. She needs to be understood. Once we connected, everything changed."
> — Mum of an autistic pre-teen

Reflection Prompt:
What expectations have you released in favour of true connection? How does your child show love or trust in their own way?

1. What moments of connection feel the most real for you and your child?

2. How can you protect and prioritise that connection ... even when the outside world pushes for compliance?

The world may not understand the way your child relates, but you do. And that connection? It's more powerful than any therapy or programme could ever be.

Chapter 8: The Road Ahead

There's no clear finish line when you're raising a neurodivergent child. No textbook that can predict what the teenage years will look like. No expert who is able to promise how independent they'll become. The future can feel like a fog … thick, uncertain, and sometimes heavy with worry.

But here's the truth you may forget in the day-to-day … **you've already come so far.**

And you've done it without a map.

You've done it with heart, with intuition, with love that has bent and stretched and grown wider than you ever imagined possible.

The Future Doesn't Need to Look Like Anyone Else's

Your child's milestones may arrive quietly, in their own time. Their passions may bloom in places no one thought to look. And the life you're building together? It might not fit the mould … but it will fit *you*.

> *"At first I grieved the future I thought she'd have. But now I see—we're building something better. Something real, and honest, and ours."*
> — Mum of a 10-year-old autistic girl

Let go of timelines. Let go of comparison. You are allowed to walk this path slowly, curiously, courageously.

It's Okay to Feel Both Hope and Fear

You may feel hopeful one day, and heartbroken the next.
You may celebrate a breakthrough, only to feel exhausted again tomorrow.
This isn't inconsistency … it's the emotional landscape of love and advocacy and raising a child in a world that doesn't always make room for them.

But you've proven, again and again, that you can do hard things.

And the beautiful truth?

So can your child.

> "There were days I thought he'd never speak. Now he tells me he loves me, in his own way, every day. Not with words—but I feel it in my bones."
> — Parent of a non-speaking 12-year-old

There Will Be Joy Ahead, Too

You will see your child light up when they feel truly understood.
You will meet other parents on this path who make you feel less alone.
You will discover strengths in yourself you didn't know were there.

And one day … maybe soon, maybe not … you will look back on these early days and realise:

You did more than survive. You grew. You loved. You carried. You showed up.

Reflection Prompt:

If you could speak to your past self ... the one who just got the diagnosis, who felt overwhelmed and afraid ... what would you say to them now?

Write it. Say it aloud. Let it land softly.

Because that version of you still lives in other parents out there ... still searching, still learning, still wondering if they're doing enough. Maybe your words, your truth, your *story*... will become part of someone else's strength.

Chapter 9: When the Village Doesn't Show Up

"It takes a village to raise a child… but what if the village is silent when you need it most?"

There's a quiet, unspoken grief many of us carry … not just about the struggles of parenting an autistic child, but about the **absence of support** we assumed would be there.

You hear it often: *"You're not alone."*

But some days, you are. Not because you choose to be … but because **the world around you has pulled back**. Friends who stop calling. Family who don't understand. Playdates that never get returned. Support that never quite materialises.

And there's a pain in that. A deep ache of **feeling invisible**, misunderstood, or quietly abandoned.

Sometimes it's not just that help is missing. It's the way the invitations fade…

The way the advice comes laced with judgement…

The way others minimize your daily mountain because they don't see it.
Or don't want to.

You realise: *Your child's needs don't just change your routines. They can change your relationships.*

The Loneliness No One Talks About

You may grieve for:
- The friendships that drifted when life got hard
- The family members who love you but don't "get it"
- The lack of practical help during meltdowns or burnout
- The impossibility of relying on anyone for a break

There's no shame in that grief.

It deserves space.

It's real.

And yet … somehow … you continue. You show up, day after day. You hold space for your child, even when no one is holding space for you.

That's not just resilience. That's love.

Becoming Your Own Village

Somewhere in that wilderness, you begin building a new kind of village. Maybe not with the people you expected. Maybe not nearby. But it starts.

You find **online support groups** where you feel seen.

You follow voices that sound like yours.

You write your truth, and someone messages: *"Thank you … I feel this too."*

You find one or two people who can sit in the hard without fixing you.

You become your own safe place.

You become the village your child needs ... and sometimes, the village you need too.

A Reminder, If You Feel Alone Today

- You are not broken.
- You are not imagining how hard it is.
- And you are not weak for needing help that never came.

You are learning to carry more than most people see.

That deserves reverence, not shame.

Even without the village... you are building something sacred.

Even without the crowd... your work matters.

"Even in the absence of the village, you rise. Even in the quiet, your love speaks loudly."

Chapter 10: Permission to Rest. Why Self-Compassion is Vital.

There's a quiet pressure many parents of SEND children carry ... the belief that they must always be "on," always giving, always sacrificing. It's easy to fall into the trap of thinking that rest is a luxury, or worse, a sign of weakness. But the truth is far more loving:

Rest is a necessity. And self-compassion is not selfish ... it's survival.

You are carrying more than most people see. You juggle appointments, sensory needs, education plans, meltdowns, and advocacy ... all while managing the invisible weight of worry, guilt, and the deep desire to give your child the very best. It's no wonder you feel tired. Not just physically, but soul-deep weary.

But here's something no one may have told you:

You don't need to earn your rest. You are allowed to pause. You are allowed to breathe.

Because when you pour endlessly from your cup without refilling it, you eventually run dry. And when you ignore your own needs for too long, exhaustion starts speaking louder than love. That's not your fault—it's a human response to burnout. It's a signal, not a flaw.

Self-compassion is the radical practice of saying, **"I matter too."**

Chapter 11: Filling Your Cup When You Have No Village.

When you're parenting a neurodiverse child, self-care can feel like a luxury you can't afford. And if you're doing it without a solid support network ... no grandparents nearby, no co-parent to tag-team with, no reliable respite ... it can feel nearly impossible.

But here's a truth you deserve to hear: you matter just as much as your child does. And no one can pour from an empty cup ... not even you, no matter how strong you've had to become.

Below are small, doable ways to refill your emotional, mental, and physical cup ... especially when you're running on fumes.

1. The Two-Minute Reset

A full spa day might be out of reach, but two minutes of silence in the bathroom with the door locked? That might be manageable. Try deep breathing, splashing cool water on your face, or simply staring out the window and letting your mind go quiet. Two minutes can anchor you when you feel in chaos.

2. Permission to Pause

If the dishes don't get done tonight or the lesson plan doesn't go perfectly ... that's okay. Grant yourself the grace to do things "good enough." It's not failure; it's survival with boundaries.

3. Micro-Moments of Joy

Make a list of small things that bring you comfort: a favorite mug, a calming playlist, the smell of lavender, 15 minutes of a podcast you love. Schedule those into your day with the same seriousness you give to therapy appointments or meltdowns.

4. Voice Notes Instead of Venting

If you don't have a friend to call, send yourself a voice note. It might feel silly, but it's a powerful way to release emotions, name your struggles, and be heard … even if only by yourself.

5. Online Connection Counts

Don't underestimate the value of digital friendships. Join Facebook groups or Instagram communities for parents of autistic or neurodivergent children. You're not alone, even if it feels that way.

6. Move, Just a Bit

You don't need a full workout to shift your energy. Stretch while your child watches a show. Walk in circles in the kitchen. Dance for 30 seconds to one song that still makes you feel alive.

7. Anchor to Something That's Yours

Whether it's journaling, crafting, growing a plant, or even building an online page … find something that belongs to you and only you. It's a quiet reminder: You are more than just a parent. You are a whole person.

You Are Doing Enough

There may be no village knocking at your door, but that doesn't mean you aren't worthy of rest, joy, or tenderness. Start where you are, with what you have, and remember: you are not alone in this invisible labour … not anymore.

You are doing more than enough. Even on the days you doubt yourself, your love shows up in a thousand invisible ways … in the way you advocate, adapt, explain, comfort, and keep going.

You are your child's anchor in a world that often doesn't understand them. Their safety. Their calm. Their home.

You might not get applause or breaks or validation from the world outside, but to your child, you are everything. You are not just parenting … you are protecting magic.

And that is *extraordinary*.

A Final Word

This journey is not easy ... but it is meaningful. It will stretch you, reshape you, and teach you how to love more fully than you ever knew was possible.

You are not just raising a child. You are raising a *whole world* where your child belongs. And you're doing it beautifully.

If you've made it this far, take a moment and honour yourself.

You've walked through stories that echo your own.

You've nodded through the hard parts, and maybe cried through them too.

You've remembered what it feels like to be seen ... not just as a parent, but as a whole person navigating a deeply personal path.

You are doing something extraordinary. Not perfect. Not always graceful. But *extraordinary*.

There is no single destination. This journey will keep unfolding.

But you have already done the bravest thing ... You have *shown up*.

For your child. For yourself. For a future you're building with love. Let that be your legacy.

With so much respect ... from a fellow parent walking beside you, with love *xxx*

Rewired

Reconnecting The Village beyond The Typical

AMELIA BRAY

A guide for grandparents, friends and extended family who want to understand, connect and support with heart.

Why This Book Exists

You're holding this book because someone in your life has a child with special educational needs or disabilities (SEND). Maybe you're a grandparent, an aunt or uncle, a godparent, a lifelong friend, or a neighbour who wants to help but isn't sure how.

Maybe you've said the wrong thing before … or said nothing at all because you didn't know what to say. Maybe you've watched your loved one struggle and wished there was something you could do to make things better.

This book is for you.

It's for everyone who cares deeply but feels unsure. Everyone who has love to give but isn't quite sure how to give it in a way that lands well. It's a gentle guide, a bridge of understanding, and an open invitation into a world that can sometimes feel closed to those on the outside.

Because the truth is:

Families raising SEND children need a village.

Not a perfect one. Not one with all the answers.

Just one that shows up … with open hearts, listening ears, and a willingness to learn.

The journey of raising a neurodivergent or disabled child is one of beauty, complexity, and challenge. It comes with joy and grief, pride and fear, fierce love and profound fatigue. And it's a journey no one should have to take alone.

You don't need to be an expert to make a difference.

You just need to be present. Curious. Willing.

And most of all, loving.

In these pages, we'll explore how to better understand what your loved one is going through, how to offer meaningful support, and how to build stronger, more compassionate relationships with both the parents and the child at the heart of it all.

This is not a textbook. It's not a rulebook.

It's a conversation starter … and a heartfelt thank you for wanting to be part of the solution.

I'm so glad you're here.

Amelia x

Contents

1. What SEND Really Means (and What It Doesn't)

2. This Is Not a Trend, a Phase or a Parenting Style

3. Grief, Growth & Grace: The Emotional World of SEND Parents

4. Invisible Load, Visible Strength

5. Please Don't Say That

6. How to Truly Show Up

7. Celebrating Neurodivergent Brilliance

8. When You Get It Wrong

9. Love in Action

10. "It Didn't Exist in My Day"

Final Thoughts

Further Learning Resources

Chapter 1: What SEND Really Means (and What It Doesn't)

SEND stands for Special Educational Needs and Disabilities … but more than just a label, it represents a wide and varied spectrum of ways that children experience the world differently. These differences might be related to how they learn, communicate, process information, regulate their emotions, move their bodies, or interact with their environment.

What SEND includes:

- Neurodivergent conditions such as autism, ADHD, dyslexia, dyspraxia, and others
- Developmental delays
- Sensory processing differences
- Physical disabilities
- Medical needs
- Learning difficulties that might not be visible at first glance

It's important to understand that no two SEND children are the same … even with the same diagnosis. Just like every child is unique, so is every child with SEND.

What SEND Doesn't Mean:

- It doesn't mean the child is "broken," "less than," or in need of "fixing."
- It doesn't mean the parents are doing something wrong.
- It doesn't mean the child is choosing to be difficult.
- It doesn't mean there's one right way to parent, support, or educate them.

SEND is not a problem to be solved. It's a difference to be understood, accepted, and supported.

These children are not defined by their challenges. They are whole, valuable, and deeply worthy of love … just as they are. They may need additional support, different approaches, or alternative ways of expressing themselves. But underneath all of that is a child with their own personality, preferences, quirks, talents, and potential.

Language Matters

You might hear terms like "special needs," "neurodivergent," "disabled," or "additional needs." Not every family uses the same language and that's okay. The most respectful thing you can do is follow the language the family uses and ask when you're unsure.

For example, some families say, "My child is autistic," while others prefer, "My child has autism." There is no one "correct" way … it depends on the identity and comfort of the individual or family.

Being open, curious, and respectful makes all the difference.

Why This Chapter Matters

When extended family and friends have a clearer picture of what SEND really means, the misunderstandings start to fade. There's less judgment. Less frustration. Less distance.

And in its place?

More patience. More empathy. More connection. Because once you understand that a meltdown is not misbehaviour, or that a quiet child is not being rude, or that a parent is not "overprotective" but tuned in to very real needs … you can respond with love instead of confusion.

And that changes everything.

Conversation and Reflection Prompt: Understanding SEND

Take a moment to reflect on your own understanding of SEND. If you're sharing this with other family members or friends, it can also serve as a discussion starter. Together, let's explore these questions:

1. What did you know about SEND before reading this chapter? What new information stood out to you, and how did it change your perspective?

2. Think of a time you might have misinterpreted a child's behavior due to a lack of understanding about SEND.

3. How can this new knowledge shift the way you approach similar situations in the future?

4. How do you feel about the language used to describe children with SEND?

5. Are there terms you've heard before that made you uncomfortable? How can you become more aware and sensitive to this in the future?

6. What are some ways you can show your support to a child with SEND in your life, even if you don't fully understand their experience? What small, loving actions could make a big difference?

7. Finish this sentence:
   I want to learn more about SEND because…

Chapter 2: This Is Not a Phase or a Parenting Style

Validating the Real Challenges Families Face

One of the most painful experiences for parents of SEND children is feeling dismissed or doubted … especially by the people they love the most.

They may hear things like:

- "They'll grow out of it."
- "All kids do that."
- "You're just being overprotective."
- "You're making too big a deal out of this."
- "If you just disciplined more…"
- "Back in my day…"

While these comments may be well meaning, they create distance instead of connection. They invalidate the very real challenges parents are navigating every single day.

Raising a child with SEND is not a parenting trend. It's not the result of too much screen time, poor discipline, or helicopter parenting. It's a unique journey … often filled with assessments, therapies, advocacy, educational battles and emotional labour that many never see.

Most families don't talk about half of what they're managing … not because they're secretive, but because they're tired. Because it's hard to explain. Because they've been dismissed before. And because they fear being judged, especially by the people closest to them.

What parents of SEND children need most is validation.

They need to be believed when they say their child struggles in ways others don't.

They need to be trusted when they say certain routines, foods, lights, noises, or environments are hard.

They need to be supported … not corrected or questioned.

Why It Hurts

When a parent is met with doubt, it deepens their isolation. It makes them feel like they have to defend their child at every turn. And sometimes, it makes them pull away from the very people they wish they could lean on.

This doesn't just affect the parent. It affects their relationship with you.

But here's the good news: it's never too late to rebuild trust.

What Support Sounds Like

Instead of questioning or minimising, try:

- "That sounds really tough … how can I support you?"
- "I believe you."
- "You know your child better than anyone."
- "I'm proud of how much you're doing for them."
- "Thank you for helping me understand more."

Sometimes, the most powerful thing you can say is, "I'm here."

Because even if you don't fully understand what they're going through, choosing to believe and back them anyway speaks volumes. It builds a bridge. It strengthens your relationship. And it lets the parent know they don't have to carry it all alone.

Conversation and Reflection Prompt: Listening Without Judgement

1. Have you ever doubted or second-guessed a parent's experience with their SEND child?
   If so, where did those doubts come from? Misinformation? Fear? Habit?

2. What is one phrase you've said in the past that you might now reconsider or replace?
   How could you express support differently going forward?

3. Think of a time when you felt dismissed or unheard.
   What would you have wanted someone to say to you in that moment?

4. How can you open space for the SEND parent in your life to talk more freely … without feeling judged or "corrected"?

5. Finish this sentence:
   Going forward, I want to create more trust by…

Chapter 3: Grief, Growth & Grace: The Emotional World of SEND Parents

If you've ever looked at the parent of a SEND child and thought, "They're so strong," ... you're right.

But strength doesn't mean they're not also grieving, growing, and learning to show themselves grace every single day.

Behind the daily routines, therapy appointments, and brave faces are emotional landscapes that run deep ... and they are often hidden from view.

The Grief No One Talks About

Many parents of SEND children carry a quiet, complicated grief. Not because they don't love their child exactly as they are ... but because some dreams have had to change.

They may grieve:

- The loss of a "typical" parenting experience
- The milestones that take longer ... or don't come
- The school experiences their child can't access
- The friendships that fade when others don't understand
- The freedom they once had
- The future they once imagined
- The loss of career aspirations

This grief doesn't mean they're not proud of their child. It means they're human. It means they're letting go of one version of life while embracing another ... often without a roadmap.

And alongside that grief?

Incredible Growth

SEND parenting stretches people in ways they never expected. It reshapes patience. It builds advocacy muscles. It sharpens instincts. It deepens compassion … not just for their child, but for others who live life outside the mainstream.

Parents become researchers, therapists, educators, and protectors … often all in one day. They find strength they didn't know they had. And they come to understand the depth of unconditional love in extraordinary ways.

This growth is beautiful … but it often comes at a cost. Fatigue. Isolation. Decision overload. The weight of always being "on." That's why…

Grace Is Essential

What SEND parents need most … besides understanding … is grace. Grace to have hard days. Grace to fall apart sometimes. Grace to set boundaries. Grace to say no. Grace to let things be imperfect.

Grace from themselves.

Grace from the system.

Grace from you.

You may not always know what to say, but your presence, patience, and willingness to sit beside them emotionally … even in silence … can be healing.

Love doesn't fix everything … but it does lighten the load.

Conversation and Reflection Prompt: Holding Space with Compassion

1. What parts of this chapter helped you better understand the emotional side of SEND parenting?
   Did anything surprise you?

2. Have you ever felt uncomfortable with a parent's grief or exhaustion ... and changed the subject or offered a "silver lining"?
   How might you respond differently now?

3. How can you practice offering grace ... not just support ... to the parent in your life?
   What does that look or sound like?

4. In what ways has your perspective grown since being part of this family's journey?

5. Finish this sentence:
   I want to hold space for the parents in my life by...

Chapter 4: Invisible Load, Visible Strength

Shining Light on the Daily Effort Behind the Scenes

When you see a SEND parent out and about ... managing their child's sensory needs, navigating public stares, juggling school meetings, or simply holding it together ... you may not see the full picture.

What they're carrying goes far beyond what's visible on the surface.

Behind every calm smile, carefully packed bag, or politely declined invitation is often a mountain of planning, advocacy, emotional strain and mental load that few people ever see.

The Mental To-Do List That Never Ends

SEND parents are constantly juggling:

- Researching therapies, diagnoses, or interventions
- Coordinating multiple appointments
- Filling out endless forms and fighting for educational support
- Monitoring their child's emotional state, sensory needs, or triggers
- Preparing for meltdowns or unpredictability
- Managing reactions from others in public or social settings
- Planning meals, routines, or environments down to the smallest detail
- Staying up late to troubleshoot tomorrow ... and replay today

All of this runs quietly in the background, every day. It doesn't stop on weekends, holidays, or birthdays. And it rarely gets seen.

Why the Load Is So Heavy

The emotional toll of constantly advocating for your child, preparing for misunderstandings, and protecting their wellbeing ... while still trying to live a full life ... is exhausting.

It's not just parenting.

It's parenting while being hyper-aware of risk, judgment, and limited resources.

And many do it with very little rest or outside help.

So when you see a SEND parent who seems "strong," know this:

Their strength is often born out of necessity, not choice.

They didn't ask to be warriors, but they became one ... for their child.

How You Can Lighten the Load

You might not be able to take the weight off entirely ... but you can share some of it:

- Ask if there's a task you can take off their plate, no matter how small
- Offer to make a phone call, fill out a form, or pick up groceries
- Be someone they don't have to explain everything to ... just a soft place to land
- Tell them you see them ... and that what they do matters

Sometimes, just being a person who notices their effort is the greatest gift of all.

Conversation and Reflection Prompt: Noticing the Unseen

1. What are some of the "invisible" tasks and pressures a SEND parent in your life might be carrying that you hadn't noticed before?

2. Think of a time when you were overwhelmed by your own mental load. How would it have felt to have someone step in or simply acknowledge it?

3. What are three small, practical things you could offer or do to ease the day-to-day life of the family you love?

4. What words of encouragement could you share that reflect the strength you now see more clearly?

5. Finish this sentence:
   To support the unseen effort of SEND parents, I will…

Chapter 5: Please Don't Say That

Words That Hurt (and What to Say Instead)

Words have power. They can comfort or cut, build bridges or create distance. And when you're trying to support a family raising a child with SEND, the language you use matters more than you might think.

Most hurtful comments aren't said with bad intentions … they come from misunderstanding, discomfort, or a desire to help. But even well-meant words can sting when they invalidate, dismiss, or oversimplify what a parent or child is going through.

Let's gently look at some of the most common phrases that unintentionally cause pain … and what you can say instead.

1. **"All kids do that."**

This dismisses the very real differences the child is experiencing. While all children may show certain behaviours, frequency, intensity, and impact matter.

Try instead:

- "I didn't realise it was that tough for them … thank you for helping me understand."

2. **"They don't look disabled."**

Many disabilities and differences are invisible. This phrase can make parents feel like they have to "prove" their child's needs.

Try instead:

- "I may not see it, but I trust what you're telling me."

3. **"You're doing too much/You're too sensitive."**

This undermines the parent's instincts and efforts, and reinforces shame.

Try instead:

- "You know your child best, and I admire how much you do for them."

4. **"Have you tried...?" (followed by unsolicited advice)**

SEND parents are often flooded with advice ... some helpful, much of it not. When suggestions come without being asked, they can feel overwhelming or judgmental.

Try instead:

- "Would you like me to help you look for information ... or just listen?"

5. **"They just need more discipline."**

This implies that behavioural challenges are caused by poor parenting, rather than unmet needs or neurological differences.

Try instead:

- "I see how much patience and love you parent with."

6. **"I couldn't do what you do."**

This can sound like pity or distance, even if meant as admiration. It may also make the parent feel isolated or othered.

Try instead:

- "I see how strong you are, and I'm here to support you."

7. **"You're spoiling them."**

Meeting a child's needs is not spoiling them. It's parenting with awareness and intuition.

Try instead:

- "You're so in tune with what they need … it's amazing to witness."

Why This Matters

You don't need to say the perfect thing every time. You just need to show up with humility, curiosity, and kindness. A small shift in language can open the door to deeper connection and trust.

And if you do say the wrong thing? That's okay. Apologise, learn, and try again. Relationships deepen through repair, not perfection.

Conversation and Reflection Prompt: Speaking With Care

1. Have you ever said something to a SEND parent that you now realise might have been unhelpful or hurtful?
   What might you say differently next time?

2. Which examples in this chapter stood out or surprised you the most? Why?

3. Think of a supportive phrase or affirmation you could offer instead … one that validates and uplifts.

4. Are there specific words or beliefs you were raised with that you're now rethinking?
   How does this new awareness shift your approach?

5. Finish this sentence:
   I want to be more mindful of my words by…

Chapter 6: How to Truly Show Up

Practical Support That Makes a Difference

It's a question so many extended family members and friends ask once they begin to understand more about SEND parenting:

"How can I help?"

The truth is, you don't need to have all the answers. You don't need to be a therapist, teacher, or expert in special education. The most meaningful support often comes from small, thoughtful actions that say: **"You're not alone."**

In this chapter, we'll explore simple yet powerful ways you can truly show up for both the child and their parents … without overstepping, guessing, or waiting to be asked.

1. Believe Them First

Before offering advice, making suggestions, or looking for "another side of the story" … just believe them.

Validate their experience, even if you don't fully understand it. Trust that they know their child best. Your belief is a soft place to land in a world that often questions everything they say.

2. Offer Help Without Pressure

Instead of vague offers like, "Let me know if you need anything," try specific, low-pressure gestures:

- "Can I drop off dinner on Tuesday?"

- "I've got a quiet afternoon … can I help run any errands?"
- "Would your child enjoy a sensory-friendly outing? I'd love to plan one with you."
- "Want to talk, vent, or just sit in silence? I'm here."

Don't take it personally if they say no. Try again another time. Just knowing someone keeps showing up is a comfort.

3. Learn On Your Own

Parents are often exhausted from explaining and educating. One of the most supportive things you can do is learn independently.

Explore:

- What their child's diagnosis means
- What sensory needs or meltdowns are (and aren't)
- What inclusive, respectful language sounds like

This shows effort and commitment. It's a way of saying, "You and your child are important enough for me to understand better."

4. Include the Whole Family

SEND families often feel isolated—not just because their child may struggle with typical environments, but because invitations stop coming altogether.

Even if the family can't always say yes, being invited still matters.

Consider:

- Planning quieter or sensory-considerate visits
- Asking, "What would make this work for your child?"
- Offering to come to them, instead of expecting travel

You don't have to plan a perfect day. You just need to hold space for their reality.

5. Respect Boundaries Without Disappointment

There may be last-minute cancellations. Changes in energy. Strict routines or unexpected meltdowns. None of it is personal.

If the family has to leave early, reschedule, or say no, meet them with understanding instead of frustration.

This tells them: "I get it. You're still welcome. You don't owe me perfection."

6. Keep Showing Up

Support doesn't always look like a grand gesture. Sometimes it's:

- A kind message on a hard day
- Remembering a therapy appointment or diagnosis anniversary
- Sending a meme, a meal, or a moment of lightness

Your consistency is more valuable than your solutions.

Love, Not Pity

SEND families are not tragic. They don't need saving. They need partnership, not pity. Celebration, not sympathy.

Show up not because you feel sorry for them ... but because you love them. Because they deserve community and joy and laughter and connection, just like anyone else.

―――――――

Conversation and Reflection Prompt: Being a Steady Presence

1. What practical actions could you take this week to lighten the load or bring joy to a SEND family you care about?

2. Are there boundaries they've set that you've struggled to understand or accept?
   How might you reframe your perspective?

3. What's one thing you could learn more about, without being asked, to better support their journey?

4. Think about a time someone truly showed up for you. What made it meaningful—and how can you pass that on?

5. Finish this sentence:
   To become a more present and helpful support, I will…

Chapter 7: Celebrating Neurodivergent Brilliance

Shifting the Narrative

In a world that often sees neurodivergence through a lens of limitation, we must become storytellers of something truer, deeper, and far more beautiful:

The brilliance that exists beyond the mainstream.

Too often, families raising SEND children are surrounded by conversations about what's "wrong," what needs "fixing," or what doesn't fit.

But there is another story waiting to be told … a story of unique ways of thinking, deep insight, unconventional problem-solving, and powerful creativity.

This chapter invites you to widen your view.

To notice and celebrate the incredible strengths and perspectives that neurodivergent children bring to the world … and to help shift the cultural story from pity to pride.

Different Doesn't Mean Less

Children who are autistic, ADHD, dyslexic, PDA, or have other additional needs often process the world differently … but that doesn't mean they're broken.

It means:

- They might see patterns others miss.
- They might hear nuance others tune out.
- They might experience emotions or sensory input with a depth that takes your breath away.

- They might question norms, challenge assumptions, or see beauty in places others overlook.

Their way of experiencing life is not a deficit ... it's a difference. And when we make space for difference, we make space for innovation, empathy, and magic.

The Power of Focused Interests and Deep Joy

Many neurodivergent children have deep, passionate interests ... what some call "special interests." These aren't mere hobbies; they are lifelines, comfort zones, and incredible sources of knowledge and joy.

Instead of trying to redirect them, celebrate these passions. They may lead to future careers, inventions, or communities. But even if they don't ... loving something deeply is always worth honouring.

Let Them Be Seen for More Than Their Challenges

So many children grow up being measured only by what they struggle with. Let's help rewrite that script.

Instead of only noticing:

- What they can't do yet,
- What makes them stand out,
- What's different from the typical path...

Try noticing:

- What brings them joy
- How they show care or curiosity
- The moments they shine, even if only you saw it
- Their resilience in a world not designed for them

Every child deserves to be seen in their fullness ... not just in their needs, but in their beauty.

Your Role in the Celebration

As an extended family member or friend, your role matters more than you realise.

When you marvel at a child's creativity instead of correcting them...

When you praise their strengths instead of focusing on deficits...

When you stop comparing them to neurotypical milestones and start loving them exactly as they are...

You help rewrite the narrative.

You help build a world that is kinder, wiser, and more inclusive.

This Isn't About Pretending It's Easy

Recognising brilliance doesn't mean ignoring struggle. Life with SEND isn't always smooth or predictable ... but neither is life with any human being.

What families need is both:

- Safe places to talk honestly about the hard days,
- And loving witnesses to the light in their child's eyes.

You can be both. You can hold space for both.

Conversation and Reflection Prompt: Reframing the Story

1. What strengths or sparks of brilliance have you seen in the neurodivergent child in your life?
   (No matter how seemingly small, name them.)

2. Are there ways you've unintentionally focused more on what's "challenging" than what's inspiring?
   What shift could you make in your language or thinking?

3. How could you become a voice of celebration in this child's wider world … at school, in your community, or among other relatives?

4. What does it mean to truly accept someone "as they are," without conditions?

5. Finish this sentence:
   To help change the narrative around neurodivergence, I will…

Chapter 8: When You Get It Wrong

Repair, Humility & Growing Together

Supporting a SEND family isn't about getting everything right. It's about showing up … even when you've made mistakes.

The truth is, at some point, you will get it wrong.

You might:

- Say something that unintentionally hurts.
- Miss an important sign or need.
- Jump to judgment or assumption.
- Overstep a boundary in your desire to help.

That doesn't make you a bad person … it makes you human.

What matters is what you do next.

It's Okay to Be Wrong. It's Powerful to Own It.

Families raising neurodivergent children are used to navigating misunderstanding. What they don't always receive is the healing that comes when someone says:

"I didn't realise. I'm sorry. I want to understand better."

This moment of humility opens the door to connection, repair, and trust. It tells the parent, "You don't have to keep proving or explaining everything … I'm here to grow with you."

What Repair Might Look Like

You don't need grand speeches or perfectly crafted apologies. Repair can be quiet, heartfelt, and simple:

- "I've been thinking about what I said, and I realise now it may have hurt you."
- "I see now that I didn't understand your child's needs—and I'd like to learn more."
- "Thank you for your patience with me. I'm trying to do better."

And then… keep showing up with changed behaviour.

That's where trust rebuilds.

The Gift of Staying Teachable.

One of the most powerful things you can offer a SEND family is a willingness to stay teachable.

To say:

- "I don't know, but I'm open."
- "That wasn't my experience growing up, but I want to understand yours."
- "I'm sorry. I said that without thinking about what it might feel like."

You don't need to be perfect. You need to be real.

Families will remember the people who tried, who grew, and who didn't disappear when it got uncomfortable.

Letting Go of Shame

If you're reading this chapter and remembering a moment where you got it wrong, take a deep breath. Shame doesn't help anyone heal. Growth does.

Mistakes can be moments of transformation ... when you choose empathy over ego, listening over defensiveness, and connection over being right.

If You're the Parent Reading This...

Maybe someone hurt you. Maybe they haven't owned it yet. Maybe you're still carrying the weight of being misunderstood or judged.

You deserve better. You deserve relationships where growth and repair are possible.

But also ... release the burden of being everyone's teacher. Let them do their own work. You are already carrying enough.

Conversation and Reflection Prompt: Growth Over Perfection

1. Can you recall a moment when you misunderstood, dismissed, or hurt the SEND family in your life—intentionally or not?
   What could repair look like now?

2. How do you typically respond when someone corrects you or shares that they were hurt?
   What might help you stay grounded and open?

3. What does "repair" mean to you—and how can you practice it more fully in your relationships?

4. Think of someone who showed you grace while you were learning. How can you offer that same grace to yourself and others?

5. Finish this sentence:
   When I get it wrong, I will choose to…

Chapter 9: Love in Action

Being Part of the Village Every Child Deserves

There's a saying you've likely heard:

"It takes a village to raise a child."

For SEND families, that village often feels like a mirage, distant, out of reach, or simply not built with their child in mind.

The village often feels like a ghost town with tumbleweed blowing by …

They find themselves parenting on islands, trying to build bridges where walls have gone up.

But **you** have the power to become part of a new kind of village. One built on empathy, inclusion, patience, and above all … love in action.

Love Is More Than Good Intentions

Loving a child with additional needs, or their family, isn't just about warm feelings. It's about how you show up … consistently, practically, and without needing praise or perfection.

It's in:

- Holding space without judgment.

- Offering help that honours boundaries.
- Showing curiosity instead of assumptions.
- Choosing relationship over convenience.

When love becomes action, it becomes visible. It becomes a lifeline.

There Is No "Us" and "Them"

If this journey has taught you anything, let it be this: There is no divide between SEND families and everyone else. These are your children, your siblings, your nieces and nephews, your neighbours, your friends.

They don't live on the fringes of society … they are society.

Creating an inclusive, loving community is not just a gift to them. It's a gift to all of us.

When we widen the circle, we all benefit from greater kindness, creativity, and connection.

Becoming the Village

You don't need to have it all figured out. You just need to start with what's in front of you.

You can:

- Advocate when someone uses dismissive or outdated language.
- Make your home more sensory-friendly for visits.
- Encourage schools, churches, and community centres to consider neurodivergent needs.

- Support policies and initiatives that prioritise inclusion.
- Keep showing up for the families who feel unseen.

Every small act becomes a brick in the village wall. Every loving gesture builds a place of safety, joy, and belonging.

Legacy of Love

The way you love and support a SEND child will ripple outward. It will shape how others in your circle think, speak, and act. It will show future generations what true community looks like.

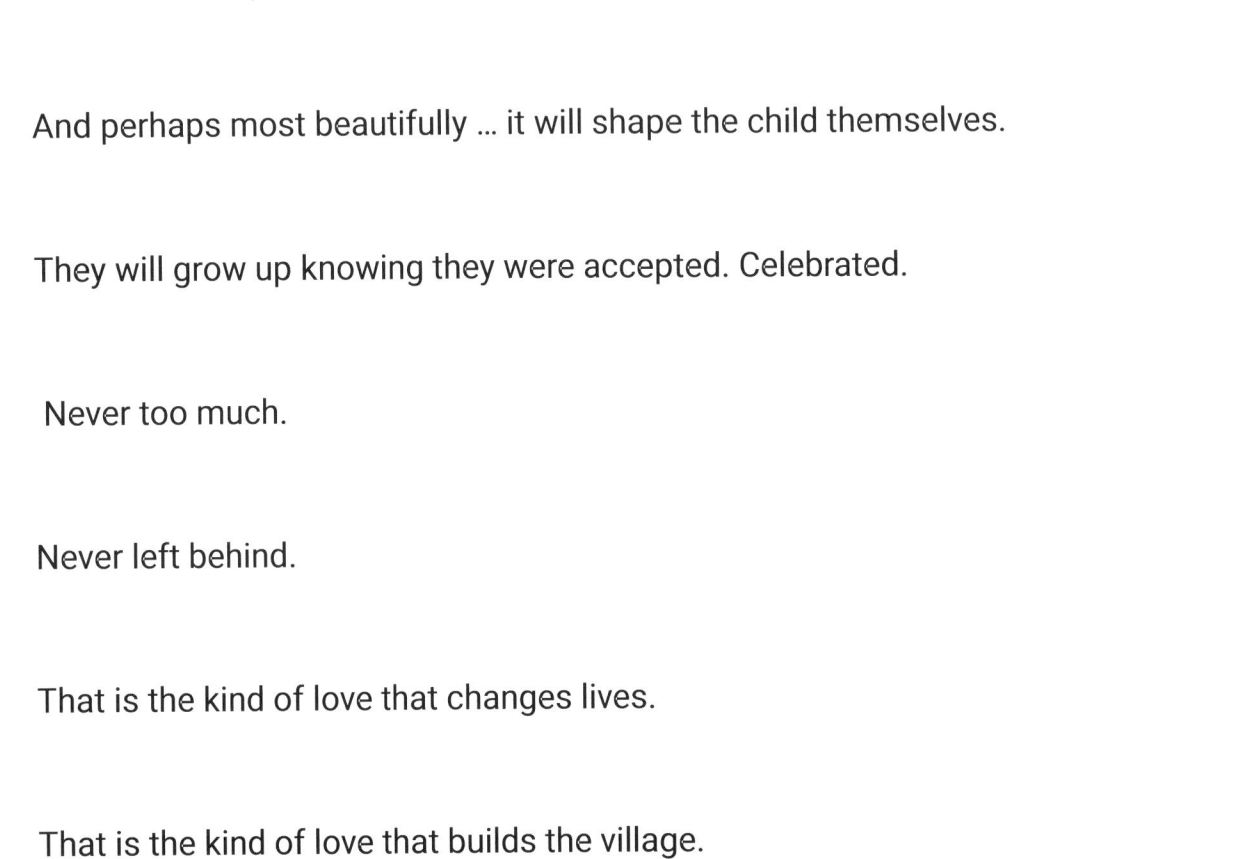

And perhaps most beautifully … it will shape the child themselves.

They will grow up knowing they were accepted. Celebrated.

Never too much.

Never left behind.

That is the kind of love that changes lives.

That is the kind of love that builds the village.

Conversation and Reflection Prompt: Becoming the Village

1. What does "being part of the village" mean to you—and where do you see yourself in that vision?

2. Are there opportunities in your home, workplace, or community to foster more inclusivity for SEND families?
   What's one small change you could make this month?

3. Who else could you invite into this journey of understanding and support? (Who in your life needs this book, this conversation, this awakening?)

4. How do you want the child(ren) in your life to remember the role you played in their story?

5. Finish this sentence:
   To become part of the village every child deserves, I will…

Chapter 10: "It Didn't Exist in My Day"

Gently Debunking Myths with Truth and Love

It's a phrase many SEND parents hear … especially from older generations:

"Autism didn't exist when I was young."

"We never had all these labels back then."

"Children today are just different."

These words are rarely meant with cruelty. More often, they come from confusion, nostalgia, or discomfort.

But to the families living in today's reality, these statements can feel like erasure. As though the struggles, advocacy, and identities of their children are somehow imaginary.

This chapter offers a gentle, compassionate path to understanding. One that honours history without staying stuck in it … and helps bridge the generational gap with truth, empathy, and love.

Autism Has Always Existed

Let's begin with the truth: Autistic people have always been here.

We just didn't always have the language, awareness, or compassion to recognise and support them.

In the past:

- **Many autistic children were institutionalised, labelled as "difficult" or "mentally defective."**

- **Others were dismissed as shy, odd, unruly, or defiant—without any understanding of sensory needs, communication differences, or neurological diversity.**

- **Some were punished, shamed, or isolated for behaviours they couldn't control.**

- **Many were hidden ... from neighbours, communities, even extended family.**

So no ... it's not that autism didn't exist.

It's that society wasn't looking for it. Or worse, it was choosing to look away.

Labels Aren't the Problem ... Lack of Support Is

Sometimes older generations express concern that modern parents are "too quick to label." But here's what many don't realise:

Labels don't limit children. They liberate them.

A diagnosis can:

- Open the door to understanding your child
- Connect a child to the support they need
- Help families make sense of what they've been navigating alone
- Protect children from being misunderstood or mistreated

The label doesn't cause the struggle.

The lack of recognition, accommodation, and kindness does.

"We Just Got On With It" Isn't Always a Good Thing

Older generations often pride themselves on "just getting on with it." And yes, many were incredibly resilient. But resilience built in silence isn't the same as wellness.

When you weren't allowed to express difficulty, ask questions, or explore differences … you didn't become stronger. You became quieter.

Today's families are choosing something braver:

Awareness. Advocacy. Community.

They're not being dramatic. They're being determined.

Breaking Cycles with Compassion

We cannot change the past ... but we can understand it, learn from it, and choose to do better.

Many older adults now realise they themselves may be autistic, ADHD, or neurodivergent ... only now finding language for experiences they've carried their whole lives.

Let's break the cycle of misunderstanding and shame.

Let's start talking about autism not as something "new" or "made up," but as something **finally being seen**.

That's not regression. That's progress.

You're Invited to Be Part of the Change

If you are a grandparent, elder, or family friend reading this:

- **Your wisdom matters.**
- **Your willingness to listen means the world.**
- **Your love, when paired with learning, can shape generations.**

You don't need to know all the terms or get it right every time. You just need an open heart and a curious spirit.

Because this isn't about blame. It's about belonging.

Conversation and Reflection Prompt: Listening Across Generations

1. What beliefs were you raised with about difference, disability, or behaviour?
   Are any of those due for questioning or reframing?

2. Have you ever dismissed a diagnosis or label before understanding its meaning?
   What could help you learn more now?

3. How did your generation handle children who didn't fit the mould?
   What impact might that have had ... then and now?

4. What would it mean to you to be remembered as someone who listened, evolved, and supported?

5. Finish this sentence:
   To honour the past while embracing the future, I will…

Final Thoughts: Thank You for Choosing to See

If you've made it to the end of this book, it means you're someone who has chosen to see. To open your heart, widen your understanding, and walk alongside a family navigating the path of raising a neurodivergent child.

That matters more than you know.

You may not always have the right words. You may still be figuring things out. But your willingness to try … to love out loud, to listen without defensiveness, and to show up without needing to be perfect … is already changing lives.

This isn't just about information. It's about connection.

The world will become more inclusive not through systems alone, but through small, sacred choices made every day … in homes, in conversations, in the way we see and speak about each other.

So thank you. For reading. For trying. For learning.

You are part of the village every SEND child and parent deserves.

A Letter from Me, Amelia

Parent, Advocate, and Ever-Learning Mum of an Autistic Child

Dearest Reader,

I want to say something I wish more people heard:

Thank you for caring enough to understand.

As the mum of a beautiful autistic daughter, I know the ache of being misunderstood. I know the sting of a well-meaning comment that misses the mark. And I know the deep, overwhelming gratitude when someone simply says, "I see her. I see you."

This journey isn't always easy. But it is rich in love, growth, and fierce resilience.

I didn't write this book because I have all the answers. I wrote it because I believe in the power of human connection to heal what ignorance has harmed. I wrote it for every grandparent, aunt, uncle, friend, teacher, and neighbour who has wanted to help but didn't know how.

And I wrote it for the families like mine … who have longed for The Village, and maybe now, will begin to see it forming.

If you've read this far, you're part of that hope.

Thank you for walking with us.

With warmth,

Amelia

Books & Resources for Further Learning

Here's a list of gentle, insightful, and accessible resources for those wanting to go deeper.

Books:

- **"Loud Hands: Autistic People, Speaking"** (ed. Julia Bascom)
- **"The Out of Sync Child"** by Carol Stock Kranowitz
- **"Uniquely Human: A Different Way of Seeing Autism"** by Dr. Barry Prizant
- **"Neurotribes: The Legacy of Autism and the Future of Neurodiversity"** by Steve Silberman
- **"The Reason I Jump"** by Naoki Higashida
- **"Parenting a Child with Autism Spectrum Disorder"** by Albert Knapp & Julie Azuma
- **"What I Mean When I Say I'm Autistic"** by Annie Kotowicz
- **"SEND in the Clowns"** by Suzy Rowland
- **"A Different Way to Learn - Neurodiversity and Self Directed Education"** by Dr Naomi Fisher and Eliza Fricker
- **"Thumbsucker"** by Eliza Fricker
- **"When the Naughty Step makes things Worse"** by Dr Naomi Fisher and Eliza Fricker

Websites and Organisations

- National Autistic Society (UK) — www.autism.org.uk

  The go-to resource for education, advocacy, and support across the UK.

- Autistic Girls Network — www.autisticgirlsnetwork.org

  Supporting better recognition and support for autistic girls and women.

- Ambitious about Autism — www.ambitiousaboutautism.org.uk

  A leading UK charity offering support and advocacy for autistic young people.

Instagram accounts:

- @autistic_parents_uk
- @happyhandswith_hallie
- @neuro_spice_all_things_nice
- @everyday_ot_ireland
- @raisingkevin_
- @storiesaboutautism_
- @werenotyourtypical
- @twins_tides_and_autism_vibes
- @elizafricker_missingthemark

Printed in Great Britain
by Amazon